Survival Family Basics

I0429826

Prepping for Violence: The Self Defense Guide to Protect & Defend Your Family When Society Collapses

Macenzie Guiver

Macenzie Guiver

Just to say Thank You for Purchasing this Book I want
to give you a gift 100% absolutely FREE

A Copy of My Upcoming Special Report "The Prepper's
Supplies Guide for When Disaster Strikes"

Go to www.SurvivalFamilyBasics.com to Sign Up to

Receive Your FREE Gift

Table Of Contents

Introduction

I want to thank you and congratulate you for downloading, *"Survival Family Basics – Prepping for Violence: The Self Defense Guide to Protect and Defend Your Family When Society Collapses.*

If you consider what is at the heart of the desire to be prepared in times of crisis and disaster, it is always about protecting the ones we love and ensuring their survival. This is one of the reasons defense of home and family is such a passionate topic for so many in the prepping community.

But many people confuse self defense with the unmitigated ability to use deadly force at their own discretion, which is a detriment to the community as a whole and creates a very dangerous environment for that prepper and their family, especially after a catastrophic event. It is important that we all embrace the idea that being willing to shoot someone over a can of beans is not self defense.

This is why I put this guide together. The need for comprehensive self defense planning and skills will be absolutely crucial to your, and your family's, survival after a disaster or other event that causes a social collapse, be it in your town, your state, or in the country as a whole. Every prepping family needs to understand what is and is not self defense and develop the plan and the skills they will need to protect themselves and each other.

This guide challenges you to question your beliefs about the use of deadly force and to consider how your personal boundaries concerning what is right and what is wrong may have to change in a post-disaster world.

From redefining what prepping for self defense means to outlining how the "use of force continuum" can be used to help you defend yourself with the appropriate level of physical force, this book will get you thinking about what you would be willing to do to protect your own life and the lives of your family and inspire you to develop the skills you will need to be prepared for violence.

Thanks again for downloading this book. I hope you enjoy it!

Macenzie Guiver

The Importance of Self Defense

If you asked 100 preppers why prepping for self defense is important, the most common answer you are likely to get is that you need to be able to defend your family and your stuff when "SHTF" day comes. While this is true, the way we are often portrayed in this area, standing with an AR-15 talking about our willingness to shoot people over a can of soup, is not self defense. That is also not prepping. Don't get me wrong, I am all for gun-ownership, the 2nd amendment, and strongly believe that for some families, firearms play an integral role in their self-defense strategy. But owning a gun and being able to defend yourself are two separate and mutually exclusive things. There can be a symbiotic relationship between self defense and gun ownership, but when we confuse the two, we cloud the issue and make ourselves and our families more vulnerable and less safe in the long run, which is exactly the opposite of what time and effort spent on self defense should do.

There is no question that self defense is important for any prepping family. You only need to turn on the news and learn about what is happening in the Sudan or Syria or wherever armed conflict is underway to get why developing these skills and mastering this kind of equipment is so important. While we live in a safer society than any human has ever occupied before us, the underpinnings of that safety can be wiped out in the blink of an eye. It only takes a few days of chaos and food or water insecurity for the rule of law to founder and for people to begin doing things they never imagined they would be able, or asked, to do. This is where our quest for self-defense capabilities must begin.

Your family's self defense strategy must start with mental preparation. Simply owning a gun, even if you are well trained in its use and an excellent marksman does not make you ready to defend yourself and your family. It makes you equipped to shoot things.

- It doesn't give you the mental awareness to know the difference between someone who is a menace and someone who is a threat.
- It doesn't provide you with the principles necessary to choose a response that is appropriate for the situation.
- It doesn't arm you with the variety of tools required in order to respond to a variety of threatening situations.
- And most importantly, it doesn't mean you have devoted the time and energy required to ask and answer the really hard questions about whose life matters more and what you are willing to do to save your own life or the life of someone you love.

Owning a gun means you are equipped to shoot things, but self defense is not about shooting things, it is about defending them. And there is a big difference.

The Goal of Self Defense

The way that "self defense" in the prepping world is often portrayed leads to the belief that the goal of self defense for prepping families is to have enough offensive capabilities, read fire power, to repel thieves, marauders, and invaders. But is that really the goal?

Most people who would be considered experts in the area of self defense would argue that this is not the goal at all. The only goal of self defense is preventing physical injury to your person or the people you are protecting. It is not about offensive capabilities. It is not about being able to guard your stuff. And it is most definitely not about sitting in a window with a rifle waiting for someone to walk into your yard so you can "get them before they get you". Don't get me wrong, I am not saying there is no place for offensive capabilities and fire power and defensive positioning when it comes to prepping, I am only saying those things are not self defense, they are ..... other things.

It is important to be clear about what is and what is not self defense because much of the prepping you need to do in this area is mental. Self defense, more than any other category of prepping, is not about the stuff. And to a large degree, it is not about learning how to use the stuff. But this is where most discussions of prepper self-defense begin, and end, with the stuff. When that happens, you can easily become distracted by the stuff and skip over the work which only means you have more stuff, not that you are prepared to use it properly.

So, the goal of self defense and the focus of the rest of this guide is the protection of your *person* and those *people* whom you are protecting. Having established that, let's get started.

Why We Have the Wrong Mindset Today

One of the greatest challenges you and your family will face when it comes to self defense is overcoming years of conditioning that will make you do everything but the right thing from a self defense perspective.

Most of us have never been in a situation where we were legitimately at risk of losing life or limb. This is not a bad thing. It means we have reached a point in human social evolution where we can exist in relative safety because of social contracts that dictate acceptable behavior and the rule of law to enforce any transgressions. Men have fought for centuries to create places where their families could walk down the street in relative safety and we are the beneficiaries of that battle. This is a gift that we should cherish, but it has come at a price.

The price is that when you live in relative safety, you never have to develop the skills needed to protect yourself from the ill intent of others. You never learn to gauge the threat another person poses or how to de-escalate a situation before it becomes violent. This means that our ideas about what self defense means and what it entails come primarily from the way it is portrayed on television and in movies. In these mediums, which are designed to sell advertising and tickets, not teach you how to protect yourself or others, self-defense involves the use of force where only cowards turn the other cheek or walk away. While fight scenes make great movies, they also lead to injury and since the goal of self defense is to protect yourself from injury, fighting and the use of physical force should always be the last resort, not the starting line.

In order to be as prepared as you need to be to defend yourself and your family during a crisis or disaster, you must first change your self-defense mindset. The hero in this story is not the one who risks the fight and wins, he is the one who finds a safe path that avoids the fight all together because not fighting is a surer path to avoiding injury and living to protect his family another day.

The Psychology of SHTF Self Defense

Working from the premise that the goal of self defense is always to protect yourself and those under your protection from harm, we need to examine what that means in an SHTF world.

Mental Preparation Matters

The first challenge we face in a post-disaster world is accepting that the world we have been living in has changed, and being mentally prepared to respond to that change. Victims of violent crime often provide their attackers with an opening or an opportunity simply because it takes their mind time to accept the reality of what is happening. Mental preparation helps you avoid that gap which creates the opening a predator needs to strike. We will discuss that concept in more detail later in this guide but for now, the key is to understand the role mental preparation plays in being ready to defend yourself.

In addition to fighting our natural inclination towards denial, mental preparation ensures we don't fall into another common trap that many victims of violent crime create for themselves. According to police officers, one of the worst things you can do when confronted by a violent criminal is acquiesce in an attempt to stall for time. Many victims believe that if they do what the attacker wants at least initially, they can buy themselves time to think of how to respond or for help to come. But in reality, violent crime, in any situation is about control.

When you acquiesce, no matter the reason, you are relinquishing some of your control to the attacker. The more control they have the less likely you are to escape, remain unharmed, and survive. Time is not on your side and when you have prepared yourself mentally for the possibility of undesirable situations and the options you have for responding, you can act quickly, rather than stalling for thinking time, when your adrenaline and fear are driving your decisions.

You need to mentally prepare yourself for the SHTF world for the same reason soldiers run drills, you want to do your thinking when you have the benefit of time and rationality so that you can react quickly and choose the best option from a range of options when a situation actually presents itself.

New Threats We Will Be Facing

In a post-disaster world, we will face different kinds of threats than we do right now which is one of the reasons we need to develop these skills in the first place. Responding to these threats will take different thought processes, decision making filters, and response options than the ones we would use to assess and respond to threats today. To develop our mental self defense capabilities, we need to define and understand these threats. While not a completely inclusive list, here are some of the most likely threats we will face in the wake of a societal melt-down.

No Law Enforcement
The availability of law enforcement personnel and their ability to respond to emergency situations must always be a consideration when pondering these scenarios. As unpleasant as it might be to consider, there is a very real chance that law enforcement and the rule of law will be absent in the immediate aftermath of a disaster and possibly for a long time after, depending on the circumstances.

This does not mean you should advocate or embrace the idea that disaster means it is time to take the law into your own hands, it simply means that you need to be prepared to protect yourself without their assistance in case they are not able to provide assistance in keeping you safe.

Impersonated Officials

Unfortunately, you cannot trust that people are telling you the truth, now or during a crisis. And while you have some safeguards against people who are pretending to be officials like police officers or military personnel now, those safeguards are unlikely to be available in a crisis. One of the lessons we can learn from history is that one of the things bad people do in bad situations is impersonate people we expect to be good in order to breach our defenses. It can be a very, very effective way of getting people to stop their car, pull over to the side of the road, and open their front door, all of which provide that same opening we were talking about before.

Knowing that this is not only possible but probable, you will need to temper your responses accordingly and set up a strategy for how you and the other members of your family will handle interactions with other people, no matter who they claim to be. If you have a plan in place that dictates your response to any unknown person, you can minimize the amount of thinking you need to do in that moment and decrease the effectiveness of this tactic.

Desperation

The unfortunate truth is that after any kind of crisis, there will be more people who did not prepare than there will be who did. As we have seen in recent disasters all over the world, when people are unprepared and suddenly have limited or no access to the resources they need to survive, they quickly become desperate and desperate people will resort to drastic measures in order to get what they need to survive. No matter how big your heart is or how much food you have stocked in your pantry, you aren't going to be able to help everyone without compromising the health and safety of your own family. But it will be more difficult than you think it will be to turn friends and neighbors away and to withhold supplies from people who did not spend the time and money before the crisis to be prepared.

How you will handle these situations is one of the hard questions you need to ask and answer as a family. Your decision, if made now, will be made using logic and rationale rather than emotion and compassion. It will arm you to do the thing that you have decided is right for your family, rather than doing the right thing based on the old rules. Since it takes time to adjust your internal compass, knowing your family's "policy" for how much help you are willing to offer, and to whom you are willing to offer it, helps you make smart choices until your compass has realigned with reality.

Gangs and Mobs
If there is anything more dangerous than the mob-mentality, I can't imagine what it will be. Even now, during the safe, civilized times we live in, the mob mentality can result in gratuitous violence on a frightening scale. People who would never consider raising their hand to another person will go along with and participate in atrocities when they are part of a larger group or mob.

When you add desperation to this picture, it becomes pretty grim. The truth is, we don't like to think about these things because it makes us wonder what we are capable of and what we would do in their shoes. And this is precisely the reason you *have* to think about it.

Thinking about the mob is how you mentally prepare for dealing with a mob. Thinking about what you would do and what you would be willing to do helps you prepare for what other people will be capable of doing or will be willing to do to you. When you understand that, you can decide what you need to do to be ready to handle it.

Raiders, Invaders, and Marauders

You might be thinking this seems like the same thing as gangs and mobs, but there is a difference between a mob of desperate or angry or frustrated or scared people and a band of raiders. The difference is moral intent. A mob of people roving the neighborhood because they are scared or hungry is a group of "good" people freaking out. A band of invaders or marauders is a smaller group of "bad" people making plans. The power and danger of the mob comes from the mob which means that individually, these people are not likely to pose a threat to you unless you threaten them first. The power and danger of the raiders comes from the individuals who, in all likelihood, committed crimes or were capable of criminal behavior before the Shit Hit The Fan.

Understanding how these groups are different isn't meant to imply that one group is more dangerous than the other, but it may inform your decision on how you will respond to a possible confrontation with each group.

As noted, raiders, invaders, and marauders are the bad guys, they are bad guys now, and they will generally be even worse guys once the threat imposed by the rule of law is removed. They are dangerous and their only intention is to do harm. While they might also want to take whatever you have, never think that giving them what they want will get you what you want; you must always assume that they will still inflict harm regardless of what they promise.

Defining New Boundaries

Boundaries are important. They are the ways in which we each define the space we are comfortable operating in. If you think of your available options in any given situation as a pasture, your boundaries are the fences that define the pasture's outer limits. They are the values, beliefs, morals, and codes we live by that determine what we do, what we don't do, what we are willing to do, and what we tolerate being done to us. Most of us would like to believe that these boundaries are pretty permanent and that we are fairly consistent in the way we live our lives but in truth, they are generally shifting as we grow and change and collect new experiences. We don't always see these changes while they are happening because they are subtle adjustments and small shifts.

But when almost everything about your world changes over night, you need to be prepared to force some major boundary redefinition and realignment immediately so that you begin operating within the boundaries that are appropriate for your new world. Not realizing that you need to make these adjustments or failing to make them quickly can leave you open to additional risk. Even worse, failing to redefine and realign these boundaries consciously leaves room for those small shifts and subtle changes to be driven by the environment around you instead of being chosen by you. This can take you in a direction you never wanted to go. They say that sometimes bad circumstances cause good people to make bad choices. Not choosing your own boundaries is exactly how that happens.

To explain what all of that means, let's look at an example. In today's world, I would never think twice about letting someone know where I live. In fact, I would be perfectly fine with welcoming someone new into my home as long as I felt comfortable around them. In a post-disaster world, I would be wary of anyone new. I would likely go to great lengths to ensure anyone I met could not determine where I lived. I would never welcome someone who wasn't part of my inner circle into my home, under any circumstances, whether I knew them or not.

While that might seem like a fairly obvious example, it demonstrates the importance of consciously choosing to redraw my own boundaries. If I had not taken the time to consider all the possible implications of meeting someone new, of allowing people to know where I lived, or of having people in my home after a social collapse, my welcoming nature would have taken over upon encountering two teenage boys who remind me of my sons. I would have been drawn toward helping them and taking care of them which would lead to me inviting them to come to the house for dinner. I would realize too late that they were not who I thought they were and that they meant to do me harm.

Understanding the Role of Boundaries in Self Defense

For simplicity, let's define boundaries as the lines that define what you will do and what you won't do. They are your lines in the sand and they play a big role in self defense.

The goal of self-defense is to protect yourself from harm. Your boundaries determine the lengths to which you are willing to go to achieve that goal. They help you keep track of the difference between defending and attacking. They help you decide when to fight, when to talk, and when to walk away. And most importantly, they help you keep your moral compass when you are presented with situations to which there are no good outcomes.

There are Worse Things than Dying

We don't need to look too far back in the history of the human race to see the truth of that statement. What those worse things are may not be the same for everyone, but by taking the time to determine what they are for you, you have taken the first step towards mentally preparing yourself to defend your life and the lives of those in your care when the world is no longer as safe a place as it is today.

The Anatomy of an Attack

One of the common misconceptions about violent crime is that it is something that simply happens. A bad person makes a decision to commit a crime and there is little that can be done by the potential victim to avoid being attacked. But in truth, violent crime happens along a consistent continuum and we can use the understanding of that continuum to prepare ourselves for disaster-self-defense.

The key to accomplishing your goal is to understand this continuum. Remember, self defense is not about fighting back unless you have no other options. Optimally, self defense is about avoiding the altercation if at all possible because avoidance assures safety. By understanding the different stages that makeup this continuum you can increase the likelihood of avoiding an altercation and minimize the chances that you will become a victim.

Five Stages of Violent Crime

The Five Stages of Violent Crime is a model that is used by the military, law enforcement, and violence prevention training programs to describe the process a criminal uses leading up to a violent attack. While this model was developed for use in normal society, there is no reason to believe that criminal behavior would change significantly simply because the infrastructure of society had collapsed. Understanding these stages will help you mentally prepare to defend yourself against a potentially violent attacker during any altercation that has the potential for violence.

Your opportunities for prevention and avoidance happen during the first three stages as this is when the potential attacker is deciding whether or not you are worth attacking.

What makes you worth attacking or not has to do with the potential attackers assessment of how "safe" you are as a target. If he believes a violent attack will be successful, he will attack. If not, he won't because he knows that if he tries, and fails, he might be the one who is injured or killed which is always an unacceptable risk to an attacker.

The reason the first three stages are important is that the attacker needs to establish all three in order to make the decision to attack. All you need to do is remove one, and you can prevent the attack all together.

Intent
The first stage has to do with the potential attacker's intent. This is the point when he switches from normal person to potential attacker. This switch happens when he steps over his own mental boundary and becomes committed to doing violence to get what he wants. Although experienced criminals will use words and facial expressions to convince you that they are not a threat, you can learn to recognize intent. Criminals display fairly consistent body language or physiological characteristics when intent on committing a violent act. Even those who have experience masking other sigs often struggle to hide these behaviors.

- Excessive blinking
- Protruding eyes
- Dilated pupils
- Raised eyebrows
- Flushed or pale skin
- Twitching of the hands or legs
- Squaring off toward you
- Placing their hand behind their head
- Entering your personal space

- Turning away from you suddenly

Most of these physiological signs are quite subtle and you may not be able to notice them consciously, but your brain is noting them so if you are getting a "bad vibe", pay attention. That is your brain's survival instinct telling you something doesn't jibe between what this person is saying and how they are acting. Assume they are exhibiting signs of intent and remove yourself from the situation as quickly as possible, if you can.

Interview

The second stage is the process the attacker goes through to determine if you are the right victim for him. Remember, an attacker can have the intent and even the opportunity but if he doesn't have a "safe" target, he won't risk his own safety, he will seek out a better victim. There are five types of interviews that are commonly used by violent criminals at this stage of the process.

Regular

During this type of interview, the attacker will be exhibiting normal behavior and will approach you for an innocuous reason like to ask for directions or to inquire about the time. The approach and request are simply a distraction tactic that allows him to gauge your wariness, assess your ability to defend yourself, and to position himself to be able to attack.

Your best defense against this type of interview is to maintain your distance, tell him you cannot help him, and use your body language to make it clear that you do not intend to allow him to come close enough to attack.

Hot

This is the opposite of a regular interview and you don't usually see this one coming. This person seems to come from nowhere and is acting crazy, screaming, cursing and acting threatening. The attacker's goal is to destabilize you mentally and emotionally so that you are more vulnerable to attack.

Your only defense to this kind of interview is to immediately and unwaveringly convince the attacker that you are committed to responding to any attack in a violent manner. Remember, he is gauging how safe it is for him to attack you and your job is to convince him that you are not a safe target at all.

Escalating
This type of interview starts out like the regular interview but the attacker quickly begins testing your boundaries with more and more outrageous or threatening behavior. If you do not stop the escalation, it will continue until he finally attacks. Date rapists commonly use this kind of interview before they attack.

Your best defense against this kind of interview is to hold to your boundaries and refuse to accept or acknowledge his hostile behavior.

Silent
This type of interview can be the hardest to diffuse because most of the time, the interview happens without your knowledge. The attacker silently watches you and uses the information he obtains to decide your viability as a target. You cannot counteract his interview because you don't know that it is happening until he attacks. The only defense you have against this type of interview is to give off the sense that you are capable of handling yourself in any situation whenever you are out in the world.

Prolonged
Where most interviews happen in the minutes or seconds immediately preceding the attack, a prolonged interview

occurs over time. This is the interview type that stalkers use. Because it is unlikely to be something you would encounter in the SHTF world, I am not going to cover it in detail here.

Remember, your job during the interview, regardless of what type of interview it is, is to convince the attacker that he will be compromising his safety by attacking you. This doesn't mean that you should act in a threatening manner or become the aggressor, both of which can actually cause violence to escalate. It means using your reaction, your body language, your tone of voice, and your posture to convey a strength and self confidence that says, in no uncertain terms, "You do not want to mess with me".

Positioning

The third phase is positioning. This is the point at which the attacker will try to get you into the position he needs you to be in and/or position his body so that he can attack. The key here is to understand that this person is not looking to get in a fight with you. They want to blitz you, overwhelm you, and overtake you quickly because if you have the ability to fight back, you might cause him injury.

Once the attacker reaches this stage, he has developed intent and chosen you as a safe victim. His only remaining requirement is obtaining the position he needs for a successful attack. If he gets the positioning he needs, the attack will happen. Positioning is often about getting you into a fringe area. These are areas where the attack is unlikely to attract the attention of others.

There are also several different types of positioning.

Closing

This is the most basic type of positioning and it is about personal space. The attacker will approach and attempt to get as close as possible so that they have the best chance of overwhelming you and quickly gaining control.

Your best defense against this type of positioning is to maintain at least 5 feet of distance from anyone you don't trust. Indicate your desire for them to stay back and take any violation of that request as the start of the actual attack.

Cornering or Trapping
This is the most common type of positioning used in violent attacks. The attacker's goal is to get you between a rock, which is him, and a hard place, which is something immovable like a wall or a car. He may also use this type of positioning to cut off your access to any exit.

Your best and often only defense against this type of positioning is to avoid situations where this can happen. You can also try to outflank his maneuver or make a beeline for the exit as soon as you sense his movement. Any time someone displays this kind of positioning, do not wait for them to attack, rush forward and try to push past them, you may be able to catch them off guard and escape before they achieve their optimal position.

Surprise
This type of positioning is intended to be a blitz assault. The attacker hides out of sight, pouncing on you as you approach so that you do not have time to thwart the attack.

Unfortunately, like the silent type of interview, you are unlikely to see this type of positioning coming in advance. However, being aware of your surroundings and paying attention to places where someone could hide can help you avoid this kind of positioning and avert the attack.

Pincering and Surrounding

These two types of positioning work the same way they just involve different numbers of attackers. Pincering is the most common type when there are two attackers and surrounding is the most common positioning type used by groups of 3 or more attackers. The goal of both types is to position you between them. Generally, one will distract your attention while the other(s) move into position behind you. They may approach together and then separate or position themselves in such a way that you have to pass between them.

Situational awareness is your best defense against both of these kinds of positioning. Paying attention to who is around you, noticing if there were two or more people who have split up, and then changing your behavior, like the direction you are traveling, in response to how the others in your vicinity are moving, is the best way to avoid being caught this way.

These are the three stages that an attacker will move through while determining whether or not to attack. As I said, your opportunity to stop the attack outright exists within these three stages. This means remaining aware of what is happening around you at all times so that you can recognize when any of these three stages are happening. If you notice one, look for the others. Listen to your gut. Our subconscious can pick up on signs our conscious mind misses. If your instincts are telling you something bad is about to happen, listen to them, don't wait until the attack starts to try to get away.

Avoidance is always preferable to physical defense!

Attack and Reaction

The last two stages are attack and reaction. This is the actual attack and the attacker's reaction after the attack. We will be talking more about how to handle an attack in a minute but before we go on, it is important to understand why the attacker's reaction matters to you and how your reaction to the attack can influence how they react.

Reaction is all about how they feel about what they have done and it can cause rapid escalation in the level of violence, like going from robbing you to raping you, and your reaction to the initial attack can trigger or fuel this kind of reaction. For this reason, if you find yourself here because you were unable to avoid the attack and unable to defend yourself from the attack, you must treat the attacker as if a continued or escalating attack is imminent, since it might be. This may mean keeping quiet so you don't provoke them or feigning unconsciousness so you aren't a fun target, but it is extremely difficult to gauge what will trigger an adverse reaction, which highlights the importance of avoiding the attack in the first place.

Defending Your Life

Two of the biggest challenges any person faces when it comes to self defense in any situation is to know when to use it and what or how much force to use. Now that you understand the basics of how an attack happens, let's work on addressing these two challenges.

Conflict Avoidance

Your primary goal in self defense is to protect yourself and those around you. This means that your first response to the potential for conflict must be to avoid it. Remember, self defense isn't about fighting, it isn't about winning, it is about preserving your life and avoiding conflict will always be the best way to accomplish that goal.

There is no room for pride at the table if the price of admission might be your life. This means that you need to mentally prepare yourself to walk away even when your pride wants you to stay and fight. Your safety has to rank higher than your image, especially after a major disaster, when access to medical care is likely to be very limited.

The basics of conflict avoidance are easy to learn and they should be in play all the time, long before you find yourself face to face with someone who wants to hurt you.

1. Steer Clear of Potentially Dangerous Situations and Locations
2. Remain Calm, Emotions Beat Logic Which Leads to Bad Decisions
3. Keep Breathing to Keep the Adrenaline at Bay
4. Project Confidence, Don't Look Like an Easy Target
5. Get Away as Soon as You Can

Evasive Action

If you are unsuccessful at avoiding conflict, your next tactic must be to evade any attack. Whenever possible, ignore the person when they engage with you and attempt to walk away. Try and put as much distance between yourself and the other person. Distance, in and of itself, can be a form of prevention. By increasing the distance, you remove one of the three things an attacker needs in order to attack – his positioning. Distance also provides you with more options and offers additional escape routes.

It isn't always possible or advisable to put as much distance between you and a potential attacker as you would need to ensure your safety. In these cases, using tactics that help you evade a potential attacker can be the better choice. Examples of evasive tactics would be hiding or circling an object like a car to keep enough distance between yourself and the potential attacker in the hopes that either they will give up because you have established yourself as a more challenging target than they expected or that help will arrive.

Situation De-escalation

If avoidance and evasion are unsuccessful or inappropriate to the situation, de-escalation is the next tactic to try. The goal of de-escalation is to slow the pace of the altercation and decrease the level of aggression in order to prevent a physical attack or altercation. There are several different tactics you can use to try and de-escalate a situation.

Verbal Compliance

Sometimes doing what a potential attacker wants, as long as it doesn't place you in greater danger, or letting the aggressor in a verbal altercation win can de-escalate the situation and prevent violence.

Verbal and Physical Dominance

This form of de-escalation can be effective in the first three stages listed above. One of the most effective ways to do this is to raise your hands in front of you, effectively creating a barrier between you and the would-be attacker, and yelling "Back Off!" or "Stop Now!" in a steady, commanding voice. This tactic can catch the potential attacker off-guard and signify that you may not be as good a target as he originally thought.

Physical Compliance

There are situations where physically complying with the attackers demands is the best de-escalation strategy you have available to you. Situations involving deadly weapons, imminent violence, or where you were taken unaware by the attack may be de-escalated simply by doing whatever is asked of you.

However, complying here does not mean that you should agree to be, or allow yourself to be, put in a worse situation. This means that if an attacker has you at gunpoint and demands your weapon, give it to him. However, if he takes your weapon and tells you he is going to tie you up, tell him you willing allowed yourself to be disarmed but that you will not allow him to tie you up. Anything that puts you in the attacker's complete control or that enables the attacker to take you or a member of your family is a worse situation and should never be complied with.

Use of Force Continuum

If you are unable to avoid, evade, de-escalate, or otherwise prevent the attack from happening, the only option left is to defend yourself with the use of force. It is important to note that this is always the method of last resort because whenever an attack becomes physical you are risking injury and death. Most self defense experts agree that the best way to approach the use of force against an attacker is to follow the use of force continuum which espouses the idea that less is best when it comes to the use of force.

While you might be thinking, if I have to use force I should go hard right out of the gate, experts recommend the opposite. The premise of the use of force continuum is that you should always use the least amount of force required to end the attack.

"Never shoot what you can taze; never taze what you can spray; never spray what you can punch; never punch what you can walk away from."

This means that the ramifications of using deadly force even after a social collapse are too great for that to ever be a starting point, unless of course your attacker gives you no other choice. Approaching the use of force this way also encourages you to develop your skills and learn to use a broad range of self defense tools.

Basically, you need to have more than firearms in your self-defense arsenal and there are several reasons for this. First, there are times when a gun isn't going to do you any good. Second, if all you have available to you is a gun, you have no other tools if the gun jams, gets taken, or is lost. Third, if you can incapacitate an attacker without having to resort to deadly force, you won't have to deal with the emotional repercussions of taking someone's life. Remember, you did not start out your day with the intention to kill someone. Having the flexibility to use multiple tools and tactics is your best chance at being able to maintain the boundaries you set around what you are willing to do and which lines you aren't willing to cross.

The tools you choose to develop are up to you but you should consider learning how to defend yourself with something from each of the categories on the continuum. Creating a self defense strategy that offers you an option at each point will give you the most flexibility in choosing how you will respond.

For law enforcement officers there are five levels on the use of force continuum but the essentials of the first two, physical presence and verbal commands, have already been covered above.

Empty Hand Control

This level involves the use bodily force without weapons to gain control of a situation. It can involve grabs, chokes, holds, joint locks, punches, kicks, and any other tactic whose objective is to subdue or otherwise restrain the attacker using only your hands and feet.

Once you have done everything you can to avoid the use of force and been unsuccessful you must decide if you are willing to use force of any kind in defense of your life. If the answer is yes, the time for being tentative has passed. Your new manta has to be hit first, hit hard and hit fast. Even though you are not the attacker, once you arrive at this point your job is to end this altercation as quickly as possible to limit the amount of physical damage that can be done.

To that end, do not let the attacker strike first. This may go against everything you think and be difficult to embrace but when violence is the only thing left on the table it is essential that you embrace it and take control of how the use of force is going to be applied. Striking first and striking hard enough to show the attacker that you are not going to be easy to control is your best available option.

Most importantly, do not hesitate. Pick a good spot in the neck, nose, knee, or groin and use a strong, powerful strike. Your goal is to incapacitate them before they can injure you.

One of the challenges of using this kind of hand to hand technique is that after that first hit, assuming that you didn't knock him down or get him to run away, your entire focus needs to shift from offense to defense. When you don't have the luxury of distance, you have to be more worried about avoiding whatever he is trying to do to you than you are about what you are going to do to him. You need to be intent on blocking and ducking and not getting hit, even more than you are on where you are going to hit him.

Empty hand techniques include martial arts like karate and tae-kwon-do, boxing, kickboxing, wrestling, and the use of pressure points to subdue the attacker.

Intermediate Weapons/ Less-Lethal Methods
This level involves the use of less-than-lethal methods to subdue and restrain the attacker. This can include blunt weapons like a baton or a club, chemicals like pepper spray or mace, and tazers or stun guns.

When you move up to this level on the force continuum, you need to be very sure that you know how to use whatever less-lethal method you pick up. You also need to be prepared for two different eventualities. First, although these methods are considered less-lethal, this doesn't mean they will never result in someone's death, it only means that they are much less likely to kill someone than deadly force weapons. Second, that they may not be enough to deter an attacker who is intent on doing grave physical harm.
That being said, sometimes the presence of a baton, tazer, or pepper spray will be enough to convince the attacker that the benefit of continuing his attack is no longer worth the cost.

Most weapons used in self defense are distance weapons which are meant to allow you to disable your attacker without having to get close enough to him to allow him to get a hold of you. This applies to all the less-lethal weapons listed here except a club or baton.

The benefit of choosing a distance weapon is that you do not have to be within your attackers reach in order to use them. However, both tazers and pepper spray are meant to incapacitate the attacker but they don't work instantaneously. If he is charging at you, it is unlikely that either of these options will be effective at stopping his charge. For this reason, it is essential that you make use of these options before he decided to charge or come in for an attack.

On the other hand, using a baton or a club requires more physical strength and a closer proximity. You also have the same challenge presented above relating to the challenge of operating without the benefit of distance. Your focus need to be on how to not get hit rather than on hitting him.

Lethal Force

This level involves the use of deadly weapons like knives and guns and should only be used if the attack poses the threat of serious bodily injury to you or another person.

Although it probably doesn't need to be said again, I think it does. The use of lethal force should always be your absolute last resort. You must feel you are in a kill or be killed situation and even after the world has gone to Hell, you need to be able to explain why you felt the use of deadly force was not only necessary but justifiable. While you may not have to explain your reasoning and justify your actions to a district attorney or a jury, you absolutely need to be able to able to justify it to yourself.

One of the most frightening images of a post-disaster world is one where every altercation results in the use of deadly force because no one ever stopped to consider that when real lives are on the line the application of force requires a higher standard, even when there is no one around to enforce it.

If you choose to include deadly weapons as part of your use of force continuum there are three things you must do:

1. Receive proper training on that weapon until you have mastered it in the eyes of a qualified someone other than yourself.

2. Learn the laws of your state related to the use of deadly force in self defense situations. Even if you never plan to use any of your self defense tactics while the rule of law is in place, it is still important to understand the law. Use this law as the guiding star to which you align your personal boundaries relating to deadly force. In essence, if you could go to jail for doing it now, it should be something you would not do when the legal system isn't there to enforce it, without proper justifiable provocation.

3. Develop skills in other areas so that lethal force is not the only tool you have in your self-defense tool box.

Conclusion

We don't need to look far back in our history to tell us that when societies crumble and the rule of law falls away, our ability to defend our own lives and the lives of our families can be the difference between life and death. We need only watch the news to see the truth in those words all over the globe. But for many prepping families, the real meaning of self defense has gotten buried under a bunch of guns and the second amendment.

But with the information in this guide, you and your family can begin asking and answering the difficult questions that will allow you to build the self defense strategy, skills, and toolbox that is right for your family.

Thinking through scenarios and considering how you will respond will help you define your own personal boundaries that outline what you are willing to do and unwilling to do in defense of your life. We've covered:

- The goal of self defense
- How our self defense mindset needs to change once society collapses in our part of the world
- Why personal boundaries may need to change after a SHTF event
- How to identify the different stages of a violent attack
- How to avoid, evade, and de-escalate an attack
- When to use physical force in response to an attack
- How to determine how much force is appropriate

From learning about the 5 stages of violent attacks and how to use them to avoid becoming a victim to understanding the use of force continuum and how it can guide your decisions about the use of physical force, I hope we've gotten you thinking about self defense in a different way. Share this guide with your family, talk about the tough decisions, explore how you and the individual members of your family will react and respond to various situations, and make your plan.

Stay Safe, and Happy Prepping!

Macenzie

Check out these other *Survival Family Basics* Titles…

http://www.amazon.com/dp/B00HG7Y4YS

http://www.amazon.com/dp/B00HYQ55W6

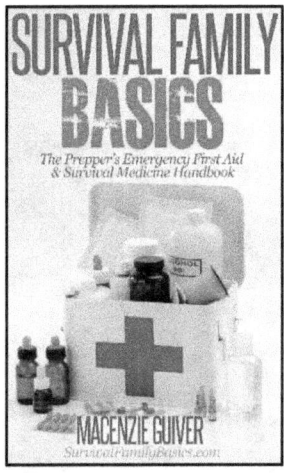

http://www.amazon.com/dp/B00I90UPSK

http://www.amazon.com/dp/B00J1V939S

http://www.amazon.com/dp/B00K00DMQE